Themes In Art *provides a fresh approach to the study of fine art. Each book is based on a theme or subject, rather than on a stylistic or historical era.* The Artist's Zoo *is the first book in this series. Within the theme of animals in art, it is possible to trace chronology and to find representatives of many of the major schools, but the first concern has been to illustrate as wide a variety as possible of artistic media, subjects and stylistic variations.*

(page i)
English Gothic Illumination
Adam Naming the Beasts
(13th century)
from the Westminster Bestiary.
Reproduced through the kindness of the owners, the Dean and Chapter of Westminster, Westminster Abbey, London, England.
Colour Centre Slides Limited.

Graphic design:
Pat Parkinson, Bob Frank

Cover:
The World of Animals, *courtesy of the Smithsonian Institution, Freer Gallery of Art, Washington, D.C.*

ISBN 0-03-926555-2

Printed in Canada

1 2 3 4 5 74 73 72 71 70

The Artist's Zoo

George Wallace, M.A.
Associate Professor of Fine Art
McMaster University, Hamilton, Ontario

Holt, Rinehart and Winston of Canada, Limited
Toronto   Montreal

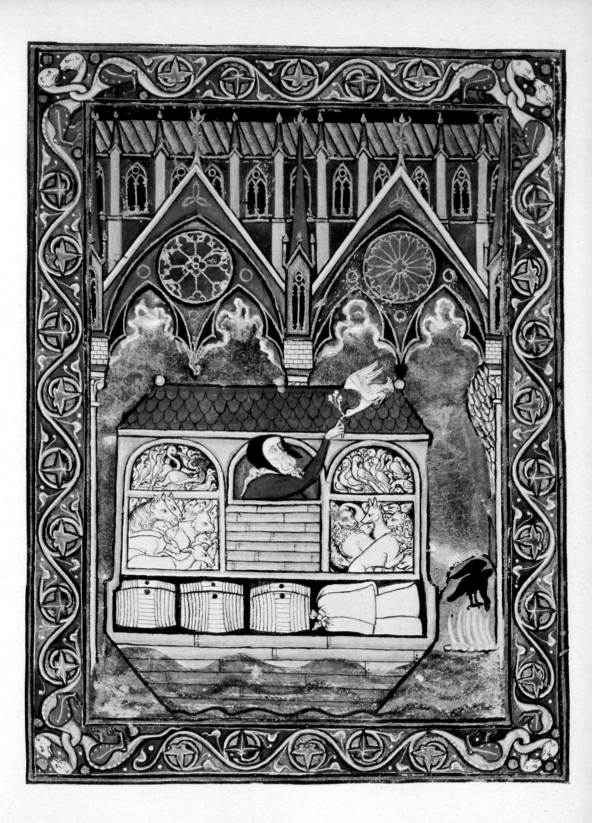

Introduction

French Gothic Illumination
Noah's Ark
(*c. 1260*)
from the Psalter of St. Louis.
Bibliothèque Nationale, Paris.
Clichés Musées Nationaux.

If you have read Gerald Durrell's exciting book about collecting animals in the Cameroons, *The Overloaded Ark*, you may be amused by this Gothic illustration of Noah, who seems to be having much the same kind of difficulty fitting everyone in. We have had the same problem in making this book, for the publisher and I were always finding "another very good one" that couldn't be left out. Fortunately we didn't have to take two of each! Even so, it was possible only to select a very few of the huge number of paintings, drawings and sculptures of animals or designs based upon animals, that are to be found in every part of the world—the work of our ancestors back to stone-age man. We hope that our *Zoo* will give you some idea of the variety of creatures that are to be found in art and that it will excite your curiosity to go and look for others.

I hope that this book will do two things as well. First of all, I would like you to realize the great variety of materials that can be used to make pictures or sculptures of animals (or, indeed, of anything else) and the ways that these materials can be worked so as to show off to the best advantage their particular qualities. For

1

just as each animal has its own distinctive fur or plumage, flight or movement, so each material—paint or crayon, stone or silver—has its individual beauty. To some extent the best artist is the one who can best show off the brightness of gold, the smoothness of stone and so forth, so in choosing our illustrations, we have tried to show artists making use of many different materials.

As you look at the illustrations, you will see that the artists have also chosen materials that enhance the particular qualities of the animals; for example, their strength or weight, smoothness or texture. Notice how the dull-shining bronze of the toad (page 50) seems exactly to suit the creature, just as the striped translucent Venetian glass makes the tunny fish (page 54) seem to be swimming in front of us. Similarly, the fine white lines and flicks that Bewick has engraved into his block wonderfully suggest the soft warm texture of the Ban Dog's fur (page 37).

The other idea I would like to suggest to you is that though these artists have represented individual animals in their pictures or sculptures, they also show us (not necessarily intentionally) their ideas about animals in general and, in fact, about all nature. Though we know a lot about some artists and nothing about others, not even their names, they all to some degree have revealed what they think in what they have made. To make this clearer, consider the following: there are people who regard animals chiefly as things to eat, but there are others who think of them as things to pray to or to study. If you think of animals as things to eat, it might simply mean that you like beef or chicken, but it may also be that you believe animals are in some way holy, or divine, and that by eating them you can share their holiness. In addition, if you believe that the souls of men continue to live in animals, you may be afraid to eat meat for fear of eating a friend or relative. In this case what you do or do not do may be either the result simply of appetite, or of quite complicated ideas about nature. In much the same way and perhaps even more obviously, the artist gives himself away in what he chooses to paint or draw. I believe that one of the most worthwhile ways of looking at works of art is to try to understand the ideas that lie behind a particular picture or sculpture. Sometimes they are very

Assyrian Architectural Relief
Servants with Horses
(668-627 B.C., dark grey alabaster, 17½″ high)
detail of The Great Lion Hunt, from the Palace of
King Ashurbanipal, Nineveh.
British Museum, London.

Gallo-Roman Mosaic
Orpheus Charming the Animals
According to Greek myths, Orpheus sang and played
the lyre so that he could charm even wild beasts and
move the trees and rocks.
Municipal Library, Laon, France.

obvious; sometimes they may take some study to work out and understand.

This is a book about artists' representations of animals, not about zoos. However, there is a connection, for the kind of curiosity that leads to collecting animals also often leads to drawing them. Zoos and menageries have existed since ancient times in China and in Egypt. We know that Queen Hatshepset (about 1500 B.C.) sent to the Land of Punt, somewhere south of the Red Sea, for live animals. One of our illustrations shows two cheetahs on leashes that were brought to the Queen.

As you will see from another illustration, the kings of Assyria kept lions and wild horses which they released and hunted in enclosures. Perhaps this was an instance of the old custom of royal hunting by which a king showed his people that he was still active enough to rule and to lead them in battle.

With the growth of the Roman Empire, animal collecting increased enormously. Octavius Augustus is said to have had a vast menagerie with more than 400 tigers, 200 lions and other African animals that included cheetahs and panthers, even a rhinoceros and a hippopotamus. As these animals came from the southern and eastern edges of the Empire and the lands beyond, they served to impress Romans at home with the size and power of their state—that it could contain such ferocious and curious creatures. It is sad to realize how many of these animals were slaughtered at improvised battles in public amphitheatres; this fact certainly tells us something about the heartlessness of the Romans. Indeed, the more you learn about these menageries of the past (and some of those of the present), the more you realize that they were characterized by great cruelty.

This state of affairs began to change in the eighteenth century with the growth of zoology (the systematic classification of animals and the study of their habits). The scientific attitude was to produce a *Theory of Evolution*, which, by showing the relation of the various species to one another and the place of man in the animal kingdom, was to alter radically our thinking about nature. It also led to a new kind of menagerie: the zoological garden. These zoos were to become not merely collections of curiosities, wretchedly housed in cramped cages, but systematic collections of animals for the purpose of educating the public and studying the characteristics and behaviour of animals in more or less natural surroundings.

This new scientific curiosity can be seen in the work of a number of artists; in particular, that of George Stubbs—especially in his famous series of drawings on the *Anatomy of the Horse* which were later made into engraved illustrations. You can see it also in Audubon's pictures of North American birds and animals where he tries to show not only their characteristic movement and flight but also their natural setting, the bushes or rocks where you might expect to find them.

As you look at the illustrations in the book, I hope you will realize that because these artists have looked at animals with more attention and sympathy than most of us do, they may be able to show us things about them that we might not otherwise have noticed. Also, underlying these individual pictures may be attitudes and ideas about our relation to animals and nature which are very important to us and well worth thinking about.

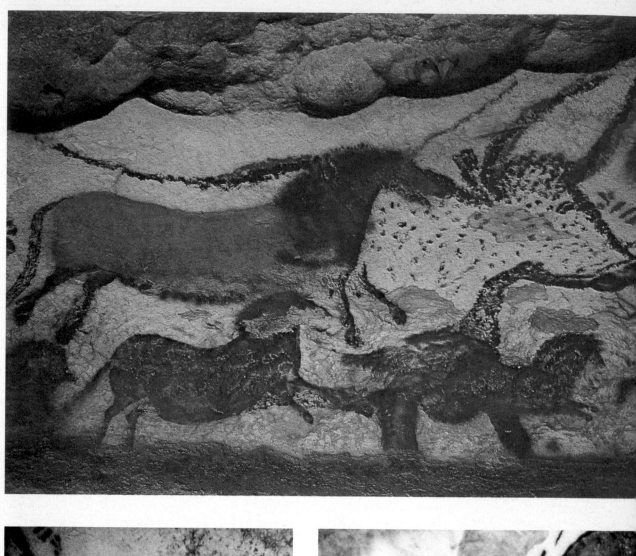

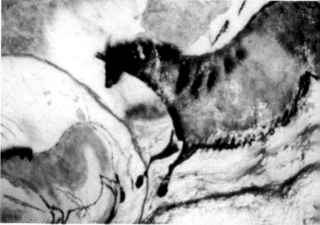

Paleolithic Cave Painting
Group of Deer
These are the deer seen to the right of the bull's head in
the previous picture.

Paleolithic Cave Painting
Two Horses
These are painted on the walls of one of two narrow
passages leading out of the large central cave at
Lascaux.

Prehistoric Pictures

The oldest pictures and sculptures we know of were made before 10,000 B.C., and many of them are of animals. Carvings were usually made on quite small pieces of bone or antler, but some paintings cover much larger areas. When the modern discovery of these wall paintings was made at Altamira, Spain in the 1880's, many people would not believe that they were very old, but thought that they were drawings made recently on the cave walls by children. It took a long time to convince even the experts that these were some of the oldest pictures in the world. The deer, cows, horses, bison, mammoths, tiger-like animals and even a rhinoceros that appear in these pictures all inhabited Europe at that time.

These paintings were made with "earth colours"—yellow ochre, iron oxides, chalk and black carbon—which were applied to the walls in various ways. Sometimes the artists seem to have incorporated the colours that were already on the cave walls into their pictures. Most of the paintings are found in dark and rather inaccessible places where the cavemen do not seem to have lived. At Lascaux, France, a cave was discovered accidentally by two young boys

Bushman Rock Painting
Hunting Scene Disturbed by Rhinoceros
(*late 19th century*)
painted on a rock at Nankluft, South West Africa.
Frobenius Institut, Frankfurt, Germany.

in 1941. This cave must always have been dark and difficult to get into, so these paintings probably were not intended for decoration as are those in our homes or public buildings.

Since the lives of the cavemen were so difficult and dangerous, it is surprising that they should have spent so much time and trouble making pictures. For some reason they must have believed that their art was very important. Experts who know most about these paintings, while they are not certain, think that they may have played a part in a kind of magic. They think that the caveman believed that by making these pictures he could do two things: first, by drawing pictures of animals, he was making sure that there would be plenty of them to hunt. In other words, by drawing them he was, in a magic way, actually making them; and second, if he drew spears sticking into his animals or if he threw actual spears at the pictures, he was, in fact, killing the real animals. By this "sympathetic magic" he was sure of having a successful hunt.

Many people have believed in this kind of magic and some do still. Though it was made

13

very much later, the scene on the Gundestrup Cauldron, which shows a man wearing antlers, holding a serpent and surrounded by animals, may represent a similar magic ceremony (page 15).

As you can see, the cave paintings are often mixed together and painted one on top of another in a rather confused way. However, though the general impression of the cave wall may be confused, the individual pictures very vividly catch the character of the different animals. Those who first thought that the cave paintings at Altamira had been drawn by Spanish children were, perhaps, being rather flattering, for I doubt if many of us, as children, could have made as lifelike drawings of animals as these. These artists show great skill in observing animals and in catching their shape and characteristic movements. Perhaps this is not surprising, for these ancient hunters had to have sharp eyes to see their prey hidden in the landscape, and without this skill they would simply have starved.

The early hunters must often have felt that some of the animals were not only stronger but cleverer than they. We know that primitive tribes believed that they could have a magical blood brotherhood with certain animals and thus take on some of their enviable qualities. Some ritual dances are a way of pretending to be a certain animal in order to bring this about. This sympathy with the animal and its movements, this ability to "feel himself inside the animal" is perhaps one of the essential qualities of all artists who portray animals.

Quality in paintings or sculptures of animals may depend on two things: on the artist's ability to make very careful observations and on his sympathetic understanding of the character of the creature he wants to represent. You can certainly see both these qualities in the art of two other hunting peoples: the Bushmen of South Africa, whose pictures, though they have all been made quite recently, are a little like those of the cavemen; and the Eskimos of the Arctic.

As you know, the Eskimos are nomadic hunters living in tents or igloos, so that they could not paint large pictures or make large sculptures. Until their carvings became popular outside the Arctic, they made small sculptures of ivory or soapstone, which were easy to carry

Prehistoric Carving
Bison with Head Turned Back
(*carved reindeer horn*)
American Library Colour Slide Company.

Celtic Silver
Man Wearing Antlers Holding a Serpent and
a Ring (tork)
(*400 - 1 B.C. silver gilt, about 8" high*)
*This is one of several plates attached to the sides of the
Gundestrup Cauldron, a large silver gilt bowl 27
inches in diameter, which was found in a bog in
Jutland. It is repoussé work, that is the figures have
been hammered up from the back. The silver has
been gold plated.*
National Museum of Denmark, Copenhagen.

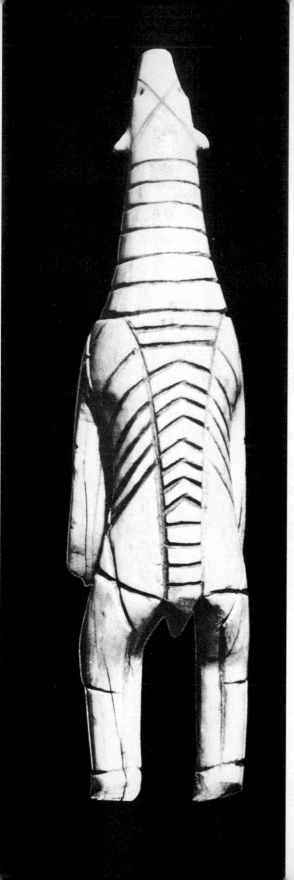

Prehistoric Eskimo Carving, Dorset Culture
Bear
(carved ivory, from Ipuitak, Point Hope, 4" long)
You can find more about these very old Eskimo
carvings in a pamphlet called "The Silent Echoes"
reprinted by the National Museum of Canada,
Ottawa, from the "Beaver", Autumn, 1967.

and could be held and looked at. We tend to think of sculptures as large objects standing on pedestals in courtyards or galleries, but Eskimo sculptures were made to be passed from hand to hand. In fact, their smooth or finely textured surfaces invite you to stroke them.

If you visit the Eskimo collection in the National Museum in Ottawa, you may come away convinced that Eskimos are some of the greatest craftsmen in the world, for with few raw materials and only the simplest tools, they have made some of the most efficient and beautiful boats and hunting equipment. I think you will find the same kind of craftsmanship in their carving.

Designs and Decorations

The Eskimo print, *The Enchanted Owl*, is very different from the carvings. One difference is that it is not for Eskimo use but is to be hung in galleries or homes of people living outside the Arctic, also, it is a "relief print" made on a piece of paper from Japan and printed from a slab of soapstone: a technique new to the Eskimos. The stone was carved so as to leave the design raised above the rest of the stone, similar to a wood or linoleum block. There are other differences. Its design is rather similar to those that Eskimo women use to decorate their clothes. This simplified and decorative quality makes it different from any of the illustrations we have discussed so far. The owl is recognizable as an owl (and a very handsome one at that), but he has been "rearranged" so as to make a graceful, curving pattern filling an oval shape. Not only has the shape been changed, but the colours have been transposed, also.

One of the interesting things about most people is their love of pattern and decoration. Men have painted or carved decorations on themselves, their clothes, their weapons, their ships and their houses. A great number of works of art are of this kind, and the object represented

in them has been stretched or compressed to emphasize a pattern or the rhythm of shapes. In the sumptuous coronation cloak of the German emperors, a pattern made from a lion leaping on a camel has been arranged on both sides of a central palm tree so as to fill the half moon shape of the cloak with a swirling but balanced design.

In this case, the shape of the cloak seems to have determined the character of the design, but in other cases, such as the door mount of a lion breathing fire, it seems to be the wrought iron that determined the swirling complexity of its shape. Of course, this piece of wrought iron, while it shows off wonderfully the skill of a very good blacksmith, also bound planks together and helped to hold the door hinges in place: it was useful as well as decorative.

The illustrations on pages 20 to 24 —though they are made of many different materials and were used in a great number of different ways— as buttons, in books or on walls—all show qualities of being both decorative and useful in various degrees.

The Irish scribe who painted the page from the *Lichfield Gospel* has contorted the animals almost beyond recognition; complicated and entangled though the picture is, a clear pattern emerges. The decoration enriches but never obscures the cross within the rectangle. This is perhaps the difference between good decoration and bad: in good decoration the craftsman may amaze us by his skill and the beauty of his materials, but his design always remains clear and controlled.

Eskimo Sculpture
Whale
(*grey-green soapstone, 9⅝″ long*)
Collection of Dr. and Mrs. Ezio Cappadocia, Hamilton, Ontario, photographed by Ralph G. Campbell.

Kenojuak (1927-   Canadian)
Enchanted Owl
(*1960, Eskimo stone-cut print, two colours printed together on one block, 24″ x 26″*)

20

Celtic Illumination
Ornamental Page, Cross Decorated with Interlaced Birds
(8th century, from the Lichfield Gospel: page size 11½" x 8¾", was once larger)
This page comes from a once magnificent Gospel Book, now badly damaged. Part of the Gospel of St. Luke and all of the Gospel of St. John are missing. Yet this page, for all its hard usage through twelve centuries, remains an almost unbelievable piece of craftsmanship. In design it is similar to other Irish books, particularly the Lindisfarn Gospel. We don't know where or by whom it was made. All we know is that it was once in a Welsh monastery which had got it in exchange for a good horse!
Collection of Lichfield Cathedral, England. Photographed by Belzeaux-Zodiaque.

Arabic Embroidery
Coronation Cloak of the German Emperors
(1133-1134, red silk with gold embroidery, 11' 2" wide)
This cloak was made in Palermo for Roger II of Sicily by Arab craftsmen, as you can see from the cufic inscription around the border.
Kunsthistorisches Museum, Wien.

French Medieval Iron Work
Lion Breathing Fire
(11th or 12th century wrought iron door mount, from the Treasury of the Church of St. Leonard-de-Noblac, France)
This has been made by cutting the red hot metal with a cold chisel and shaping it with a hammer.
The Metropolitan Museum of Art,
The Cloisters Collection, 1947.

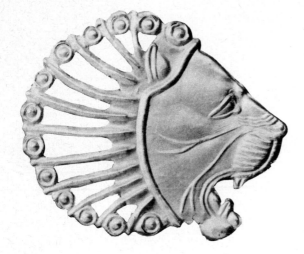

Achaemenian (Persian) Gold
(c. 400 B.C., gold repoussé, the largest is 2″ x 2¼″)
These placquettes have little loops on the back of them
and were probably sewn onto clothing.
Royal Ontario Museum, Toronto.

French-Canadian Iron Work
Chanticleer
(19th century, sheet iron)
This is a good example of the many fine weather
cocks that were made in the Province of Quebec.
Royal Ontario Museum, Toronto.

African Ivory from Benin, Nigeria
Leopard
(c. 16th or 17th century, ivory with copper studs)
British Museum, London.

Sassanian (Persian) Silver
King Peroz Shooting Ibexes with Bow and
Arrow
(5th century, cast silver, engraved and embossed,
8⅝" diameter)
Some areas have been gilded to give a contrast of
colour.
Fletcher Fund, Metropolitan Museum of Art,
New York.

Pre-Columbian Inca Silver from Peru
Alpaca
(1450-1540, silver repoussé, 9 7/16" high)
American Museum of Natural History, New York.

Australian Aboriginal Painting
Two Kangaroos
(20th century from Oenpelli, Australia, paint
on tree bark, 40¾" x 25")
The strange thing about this painting is that the
artist has not merely shown what he could see of the
outside of the animals, but also what he knew to be
inside them.
Photograph courtesy of UNESCO.

The Zoo

This section contains a series of illustrations with the different kinds of animals arranged in groups so that you can compare them.

As you come to know more about the history of art, you will realize that there have been times when artists were interested in looking at the world around them, just as there have been other times when they were not. The Renaissance in the fifteenth century is, among other things, the beginning of a period of great curiosity which has continued up to the present. You might expect artists during that time to use drawing and painting as a way of looking at things.

One architectural historian makes drawings of the Italian buildings he studies, because then, as he explains, he has to look at them very carefully. Thus he discovers things about them which he would not notice if he simply took a photograph. This is drawing as a way of learning.

Drawing can also be a way of showing or pointing out, since the artist, precisely because he has looked attentively, may be able to show clearly in his drawing how the parts fit together and how it all works. This is why looking at a good drawing can sometimes be more informative than looking at the real thing. I think that this is one of the attractive things about European or Western paintings and drawings since the Renaissance—so you will not be surprised that more than half of our illustrations in *Artist's Zoo* belong to this Western tradition.

Antoine Louis Barye, (*1796-1875, French*)
Tiger
(*1836, bronze, 15¾″ long*)
Barye was particularly fascinated by the strength and ferocity of the carnivorous animals and many of his sculptures emphasize these qualities by showing animals fighting.
Art Gallery of Hamilton, Ontario.

31

Pisanello (c. 1395-c. 1455, Italian)
Cheetah Springing to the Right
(c. 1445, pen and water colour on parchment,
6⅜″ x 9⅛″)
It is interesting to compare Pisanello's drawing with
the Egyptian relief on page 3. Because over short dis-
tances they are the fastest of all animals, and because
they are easily tamed, cheetahs have been used to hunt
deer since ancient times.

Parchment is sheep, goat or calf skin, that has been
scraped and prepared to make a smooth, flexible,
ivory-coloured sheet. Before the large scale manufac-
ture of paper in Europe in the 15th century it was used
to draw and to write upon. Vellum is a superior kind
of parchment made from calf skins, which was used
in medieval books.
Cabinet des Dessins, Musée du Louvre.

Chinese Ceramic, Wei Dynasty
Horse with Saddle
(386-535, grey clay with traces of polychrome, 9½"
high)
This proud and beautiful horse is part of a group of
figures and animals from a grave.
Royal Ontario Museum, Toronto.

Rembrandt van Rijn (1606-1669, Dutch)
Lioness Devouring a Bird
(c. 1641, black chalk with grey washes heightened
with white on dark brown paper, 5" x 9 7/16")
British Museum, London.

Mughal Painting, India
Zebra
(*17th century, black and white drawing, halter coloured red, 3⅝" x 4½"*)
Courtesy Museum of Fine Arts, Boston, Goloubew Collection.

Thomas Bewick (*1753-1828, English*)
Ban Dog
(*c. 1790, wood engraving, 2 1/16" x 3¼"*)
Bewick says of the Ban dog that it is smaller, more active and vigilant than the mastiff. It had yellowish-grey hair streaked with black or brown.
Mills, Memorial Library, McMaster University, Hamilton, Ontario.

Celtic Bronze
Boar
(*c. 1st century B.C., cast bronze, 26¾″ high x 49⅝″ long*)
To the Celts, the wild boar was a sacred animal of the underworld, so that this sculpture may have had some religious meaning. At the time of the Roman conquest of Gaul it was hidden under the bank of the Loire River.
Orléans, Musée Historique, France.

Ancient Egyptian Bronze
Cat
(Probably of the Roman Period, cast bronze with nose ring and earrings of gold, 13" high)
This is the animal image of the cat-headed goddess.
Bastet.
British Museum, London.

Gerhard Marcks (1889-   German)
The Big Cats
(1921, woodcut, 11½" x 15¼")
Courtesy of the Fogg Art Museum, Harvard University.

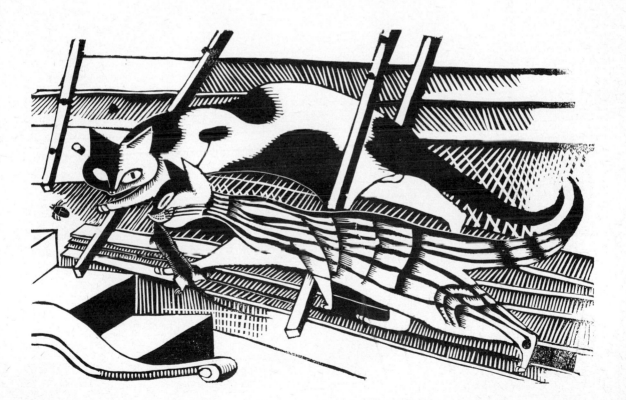

Albrecht Dürer (1471-1528, German)
A Hare
(1502, water colour, 9⅞″ x 8⅞″)
Erich Lünemann, Albertina, Wien.

Henri Toulouse-Lautrec (1864-1901, French)
Les Lapins
(1899, lithograph)
At his own suggestion Lautrec made twenty-two full-page lithographs and six decorative tailpieces for Jules Renard's book, "Histoires Naturelles", which was published in 1899. He spent many hours in the zoos of the Jardin d'Acclimatation and the Jardin des Plantes, studying and drawing the animals.
Harvard College Library, Department of Printing and Graphic Arts.

Paul Fournier (1939-   *Canadian*)
Bulldog Bat
(1966, *detail of pen drawing, detail illustrated :*
5½″ x 8″)

Hans Holbein the Younger (1497/8-1543, *Swiss*)
The Bat
(*brush and wash drawing with water colour
lightly applied,* 6½″ x 9″)
*Öffentliche Kunstsammlung, Kupferstichkabinett,
Basel.*

Jacob de Gheyn II (1565-1629, Dutch)
Studies of a Field Mouse
(*pen and brush drawing in grey ink 5 1/16" x 7 3/16"*)
Rijksmuseum Printroom, Amsterdam.

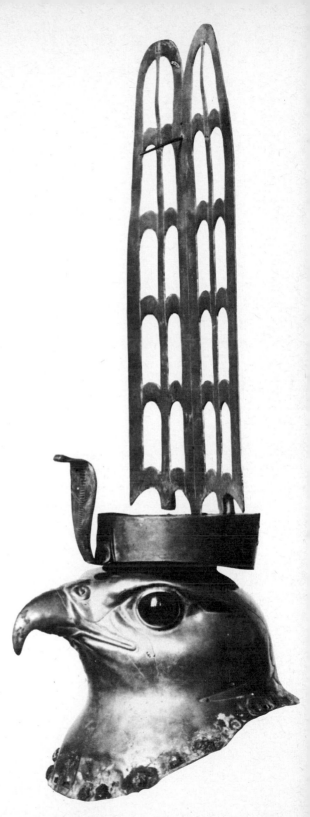

Henri Gaudier-Brzeska (1891-1915, French)
Vulture
(*pen and ink, 15" x 10"*)
National Gallery of Canada, Ottawa.

Ancient Egyptian Gold
Falcon's Head
(*c. 2700 B.C., gold repoussé, 14¼" high*)
Egyptian Museum, Cairo.

45

1508

Albrecht Dürer (1471-1528, German)
The Owl
(1508, pen and brush drawing, 7½″ x 5½″)
Albertina, Vienna.
American Library Colour Slide Company.

Greek (Proto-Corinthian) Ceramic
Owl
(c. 650-625 B.C., painted and moulded pottery
perfume bottle)
Louvre, Paris. Clichés Musées Nationaux.

Owls
(c. 1700, pen drawing with water colour)
from the "Codex Canadencis", which perhaps was
made by Abbé Louis Nicolas. This remarkable manu-
script book is an attempt to make a pictorial inventory
of the French possessions in the New World. It contains drawings of Indian life and customs and of the
plant, birds and wild animals of Canada and was
probably made towards the end of the 17th century.
Collection of the Thomas Gillcrease Institute,
Tulsa, Oklahoma.

Greek Sculpture
Cockerel
(late 6th century B.C., grey limestone relief,
16½" high)
This carving comes from Xanthus in South West
Turkey.
British Museum, London.

La petite chouette

p. 51.

f. 68

autre chouette

chatuant

L

Andrea Riccio (1470-1532, Italian)
Crab
(Italian Renaissance black lacquer over reddish-
brown bronze, 6¾" wide)
This is a small box with a hinged lid. Lacquer is a
shellac-based paint which is often hardened by baking.
Samuel H. Kress Collection, National Gallery
of Art, Washington, D.C.

Italian Renaissance Bronze
Toad
(Paduan, early 16th century, bronze with dark
brown patina, 1¾" high)
This was probably part of a table fountain or perfume
burner. "Patina" is the discolouration that usually
forms on the surface of bronze after a long time. It is
caused by impurities in the air or from the bronze
having been in the sea or simply from its being
handled. The patina is usually green, blue, brown or
black or a combination of these colours. It may be
rough and crusty or smooth in texture. It is now
frequently produced artificially with chemicals and
heat.
Samuel H. Kress Collection, National Gallery
of Art, Washington, D.C.

Australian Aboriginal Painting
Constellation of Orion and the Pleiades
and Mangrove Crabs
(bark painting)
From the Gulf of Carpentaria, Arnhemland, North-
ern Australia. The Australian aborigines make a
variety of paintings. They are still making bark
paintings and within living memory were making
cave paintings. Some of these pictures seem to be made
just for the pleasure of making them, but some were
used for magic. The bark used comes from the euca-
lyptus tree. Very few colours are used—black, red,
yellow and white—and are fixed with the juice from
orchid bulbs. The painting is done with small sticks,
pieces of bone and brushes made from strips of chewed
bark.
Photograph courtesy of UNESCO.

53

Venetian Glass
Tunny Fish
(*19th century, blown glass*)
By courtesy of the Victoria and Albert Museum,
London.

English Wood Engraving
John Dory
(*c. 1800, wood engraving, actual size*
2¾″ x 2⅜″)
This engraving was possibly made by
Thomas Bewick's son, John.

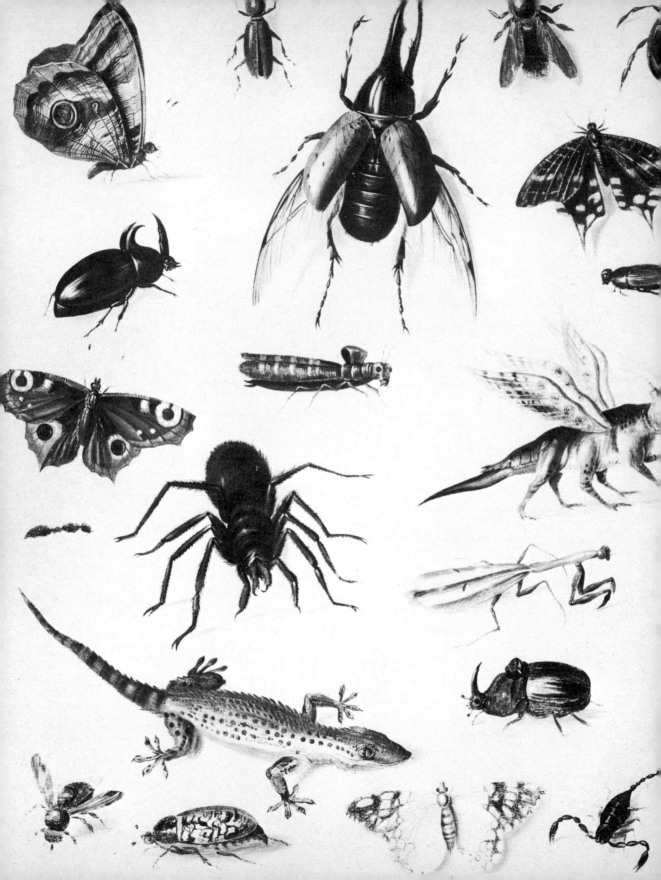

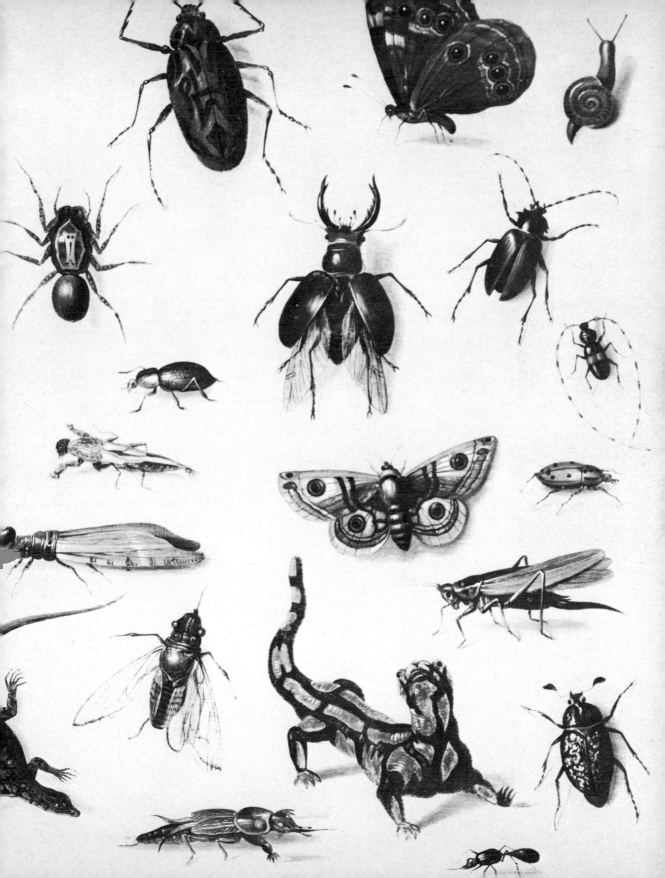

Jan van Kessel (1626-1779, Flemish)
Insects and Reptiles
(water colour)
This picture seems to show the beginning of a scientific interest, for the artist is curious about these unusual creatures and makes careful well-observed drawings of them. However, he has no idea about classifying them or grouping them according to their similarities; all that impresses him is their strangeness, and the one in the middle is certainly that.
Rheinisches Landesmuseum, Bonn, Germany.

English Wood Engraving
Dragon Fly
(c. 1800, wood engraving, 1¾" x 1¾")

Thomas Bewick (1753-1828, English)
The Bee
(c. 1797, wood engraving, 1 1/16" wide)
Mills Memorial Library, McMaster University, Hamilton, Ontario.

58

Maria Sibylle Merian (1647-1717, *Dutch*)
Study of Plant and Insects
(*c. 1696, water colour, 10 1/16" x 14"*)
Madam Merian was a very celebrated painter of
plants and insects. She travelled with her daughter
to Surinam (Dutch Guiana) to find new tropical
specimens. In some cases the Indians, who collected
for her, cheated by sticking pieces from several insects
together to make new ones specially for her.
Prentenkabinet, Kunsthistorisch Instituut,
Rijksuniversiteit, Leiden, Holland.

Leonard Baskin (1922-   *American*)
Porcupine
(1951, woodcut, 19″ x 25⅜″)
Collection of Mr. and Mrs. J. A. McCuaig,
Hamilton, Ontario.

The Curiosities

Menageries have always thrived on strange and unusual-looking animals, the odder the better. Conrad Gesner's porcupine is of this kind and his book, *Icones Animalium*, contains not only woodcuts of some very odd-looking animals, which one would doubt he had actually seen, but also prints of a number of monsters of the Siamese-twin or two-headed-calf variety.

Albrecht Dürer's woodcut of a rhinoceros is a similar "wonder." This animal had been brought to Lisbon and in 1515 was offered by King Manuel of Portugal to the Emperor Maximilian. Dürer was hoping to make a little money from people's curiosity about the strange royal present and made a print of it. His woodcut was a great success and was frequently copied, even though it was zoologically inaccurate. Indeed, when Europeans began to see rhinoceri for themselves, they seem to have been a little puzzled that the animals didn't look more like Dürer's print. Dürer, in fact, had never seen this animal. He had drawn his picture from a brief description and someone else's rough sketch and tells in his caption of a fight between an elephant and "this quick, lively and cunning animal!"

Albrecht Dürer (1471-1528, German)
Rhinoceros
(1515, woodcut, 8⅜" x 11⅞")
The Metropolitan Museum of Art, New York.
Gift of Harry G. Friedman, 1959.

The Artist Takes a Closer Look

At the end of the eighteenth century there was a great interest in natural history and many illustrated books on animals, birds, insects and plants were produced. A large number of George Stubb's pictures are portraits of race-horses, but he also made pictures of wild animals. All his pictures, but particularly his horse paintings, show his knowledge of anatomy. Stubbs had spent several years making dissections of horses to get the information for his book, *The Anatomy of the Horse*. Not only was he interested in knowing the correct position of the bones and muscles and how they were articulated, but as you can see in the *White Horse Frightened by a Lion* he was also one of the first artists to be curious about an animal's expression: how it changed its stance and appearance when it was frightened or angry. This was also to be particularly interesting to artists of the next generation such as Géricault, Delacroix and Barye.

A similar effort to make accurate and detailed illustrations is characteristic of Thomas Bewick and John James Audubon. Bewick's black-and-white illustration of a Yellow Bunting is a wood engraving — a technique for print making which he seems to have invented, or at least largely developed.

Audubon, a Frenchman who came to America as a young man, had been interested in drawing birds since his school days. He travelled all over America to study them and, as you can see from his picture of the *Orchard Oriole*, he was very clever not only at painting the shape and colour of the various birds, but at showing their characteristic movements. In 1826 Audubon brought to England 240 of his watercolours which he exhibited with great success in various cities. His intention in coming to England was to have his pictures made into illustrations for a book, for the finest engravers were then working in England and France. He came to an arrangement with Robert Havell Jr., who made from his pictures full-scale plates in etching and aquatint. The black-and-white prints from these plates were watercoloured by hand—a very slow way of making book illustrations. It took almost ten years to produce the *Birds of America*, one of the most handsome natural history books ever made. It contained 435 of these large and beautiful illustrations.

The three pictures of Audubon's *Shearwater*

George Stubbs (1724-1806, *English*)
A Skinned Horse
(*c. 1776, black chalk on paper, 7⅛″ x 14¼″*)
This is one of a series of drawings of various stages of
the dissection of a horse which was used to illustrate
his book on the anatomy of horses.
Royal Academy of Arts, London.

George Stubbs (1724-1806, *English*)
Common Fowl
(*1804, engraving*)
British Museum, London.

TAB. X.

George Stubbs (1724-1806, *English*)
White Horse Frightened by a Lion
(1770, *oil painting*, 39¾" x 50⅛")
Walker Art Gallery, Liverpool, England.

Thomas Bewick (1753-1828, *English*)
Yellow Bunting
(*c. 1797, wood engraving, 2 3/16" x 3¼"*)
Illustration from Bewick's
"History of British Birds", 1797.
Mills Memorial Library, McMaster University,
Hamilton, Ontario.

show how this artist set about his work. In 1826
Audubon sailed from New Orleans for England
in the ship "Delos." Becalmed in the Gulf of
Mexico near the west coast of Florida, he saw
great numbers of these birds. As you can tell
from one of the notes on the drawing, the
ship's mate killed four of them with one shot
and from one of these, Audubon made a life-
sized drawing. He had developed his own careful system of measuring birds and added written
notes on the proportions of particular parts of
this bird and on the colour of its plumage,
beak, eyes and legs. The watercolour painting
which shows the bird swimming on the sea
was not made until several years later, possibly
not until 1835. Sometimes Audubon wrote
notes on the margins of the paintings, telling
Robert Havell of changes he wanted made in
the plates. Sometimes two or more paintings
were combined in one illustration. Though he
seemed to have been very satisfied with the
etched plates of Havell, he was occasionally
very upset by the unreliability of the colourists
who worked on the prints, and he was able to
maintain a suitable standard only by having his
wife, one of his sons or himself supervise their
work.

John James Audubon (1785-1851, American)
Audubon's Shearwater
(1826, life-size pencil drawing on a page of
Audubon's Journal)
Yale University Library.

John James Audubon (1785-1851, American)
Audubon's Shearwater
(c. 1835, water colour)
New-York Historical Society, New York.

Robert Havell Jr. (English).
Dusky Petrel, Puffinus Obscurus,
Male In Spring
(1836, etching and aquatint with water colour,
12¼" x 19½")
Metropolitan Central Library, Toronto,
photographed by Ralph G. Campbell.

Dusky Petrel
PUFFINUS OBSCURUS
Male in Spring

Orchard Oriole.— 1 & 2. males
plumage—
Icterus spurius   3 & 4. males
and third
Plant Vulgo Honeylocust   females
th. all bird

No. 9. plate 42.—
Published 1828.—
London.   John J A

Louisiana [?]

Animals in Motion

John James Audubon (1785-1851 , American)
Orchard Oriole
(1822, water colour on paper)
This was painted in Louisiana April 12, 1822. The
nest and the honey locust branch were probably
painted by Joseph Mason, who was working for
Audubon at that time.
New-York Historical Society, New York.

Except for King Ashurbanipal's Lions (page 5) and Audubon's *Orchard Oriole* (page 70), most of the animals in *Artist's Zoo* are uncharacteristically still, unlike so many animals in real zoos that pace restlessly about in their cages. Until the invention of the movie camera, it was impossible to show movement and all the painter or sculptor could do was to suggest by stance and gesture that the animal was moving. An unknown Gallic sculptor (page 74) has achieved this suggestion of motion in the headlong leap of his bronze dog. Théodore Géricault has made us realize it in his beautiful drawing of the sensuous squirmings of his cat.

Another way of picturing movement is to present a series of images and let the viewer reconstruct the in-between movements in his imagination from these "stills." This is what Giacomo Balla has done in his picture *Dog on a Leash*. What is attractive about this picture is that it not only shows movement, but also how the repeating shapes of legs, chains and skirts fit together in a pleasing pattern. It is hard to believe that Balla would have thought of this design if he had not seen multiple-exposure photographs or early movies.

The large number of photographs (there were more than 800 of them) Eadweard Muybridge made of the movements of human beings and animals was the first systematic attempt to compare the movements of one animal with another. Muybridge showed great ingenuity in his use of batteries of cameras, for, in most cases, he simultaneously photographed the movement of his subject from three different directions. Though his photographs were sponsored by the Department of Comparative Anatomy at the University of Philadelphia's medical school, they have fascinated painters and sculptors for the last eighty years.

Théodore Géricault (*1791-1824, French*)
Studies of a Wild Striped Cat
(*pencil drawings on paper, 12½″ x 15¾″*)
Courtesy of the Fogg Art Museum, Harvard University, Grenville L. Winthrop Bequest.

72

74

Gallo-Roman Bronze
Running Dog
(bronze cast, 2⅛" high x 4¾" long)
Historical Museum, Berne, Switzerland.
Photograph by Bernese Historical Museum.

Giacomo Balla, (1874-   Italian)
Dog on a Leash
(1912, oil colour on canvas, 35⅜" x 42½")
George F. Goodyear and the Fine Arts Academy,
Buffalo.

Eadweard Muybridge (1830-1904, English)
Cat in Trot Changing to Gallop *(1884-85)*
George Eastman House Collection, Rochester,
New York.

English Gothic Sculpture
Sow Suckling her Farrow
(*c. 1280-1370, boss carved on keystone of a vault of Exeter Cathedral*)
Most Gothic cathedrals are decorated with an amazing quantity of sculpture. When you visit these churches, you immediately notice the large and impressive pieces, but after a time you become aware that there are also many smaller sculptures showing more everyday scenes like this one of the sow and her litter. In a real sense these churches are the Arks of God with room for even the humblest creatures inside.
Courtesy the National Monuments Record, London.

Animal Pictures as Parables

When George Grosz, a German artist who had been driven from his homeland by the Nazis, made these drawings of a dead mouse, I think he was doing more than recording an accident to a mouse— more even than telling us that he felt sorry for the little creature as he saw it strangled in the trap. I think he saw the trapped mouse as a symbol of himself and other men. This picture is a parable in so far as it has more meaning than is at first obvious. Whether or not I am correct in thinking of George Grosz's drawing as a parable, it is surely true of Holman Hunt's *Scapegoat*, of the anonymous *Jonah and the Whale* and of Peter Bruegel's proverb of the *Greater Fish Eating the Smaller*. In each case you see a picture or carving of an animal which is very attractive in itself but which has a larger meaning. The second meaning is fairly obvious in the case of the *Greater Fish*, but in the case of the others, you may have to look in the Bible to discover what the artist is thinking about. This "story within a story" is, of course, an aspect of a great many pictures, not just those dealing with animals.

George Grosz (1893-1959, German)
Mouse in a Trap
(1950-51, pencil on white paper, 9¼″ x 6″)
a page from a sketch book.
Courtesy of the Fogg Art Museum, Harvard University, Anonymous Gift.

William Holman Hunt (1827-1910, English)
The Scapegoat
(1854, oil colour on canvas, 33½″ x 54″)
The Trustees of the Lady Lever Collection, Port Sunlight, England.

Italian Romanesque Sculpture
Jonah and the Whale
(*c. 1260, marble relief*)
Cathedral, Sessa Aurunca.
Gallerie de Napoli, Italy.

Peter Bruegel (1525/30-1569, Flemish)
The Greater Fish Eating the Smaller
(*pen drawing, 8½″ x 11⅞″*)
Erich Lüneman, Albertina, Wien.

Eskimo Sculpture by Pitsoolak of Pound Inlet
Sedna, Goddess of Sea Animals
(*dark grey soapstone, 8¼″ long*)
Collection of Dr. and Mrs. Ezio Cappadocia, Hamilton, Ontario, photographed by Ralph G. Campbell.

Fabulous Beasts

As I said earlier, artists have often worked for scientists, making careful, detailed illustrations of various animals to show their colour and texture, the arrangement of their muscles or the shape of their skeletons. However, they have also made pictures of quite a different kind, ones that illustrate creatures of the imagination. Such are the beasts that you sometimes find described in folk tales or that travellers, back from long voyages, invented to impress the people at home. Most of these creatures were made by combining parts of various real animals and, as you might expect, were supposed to have many dangerous and magical qualities. I have chosen illustrations of three such beasts because in their different ways they seem to me to be very handsome and decorative creatures.

Paul Klee is perhaps doing something of a different kind in his "magic picture." It is a little like a small aquarium, but he has put some very unusual fish in it, so that it is like something you might see in a strange, but quite pleasant dream.

I don't know if you can say the same about Giuseppi Arcimboldo's extraordinary visual

Gothic Illumination
Whale
(*from the Westminster Bestiary, 13th century, glare painting on parchment*)
This soulful looking creature is, in fact, much more like a walrus than a whale.
Reproduced through the kindness of the owners, the Dean and Chapter of Westminster, Westminster Abbey, London, England.
Colour Centre Slides Limited.

joke; it is rather a nightmare. Yet you tend to smile at the cleverness with which he has painted all the different fish and the skill with which he has fitted them together to make a head. He did this kind of thing a great many times with different groups of things, sometimes using fruit, another time flowers or guns, to make heads.

Edward Lear, who made our final illustration, drew some very odd creatures to illustrate his nonsense poems, but he was also a good draughtsman of real animals. When he was still at school, his father died, leaving very little money, but Lear was able to support the family by making drawings of the parrots and turtles at the London Zoo.

Etruscan Bronze
Chimera
(*5th century, B.C., bronze cast, 31½" high*)
Archaeological Museum, Florence.
American Library Colour Slide Company.

Paul Klee (1879-1940, *Swiss*)
Fish Magic
(*1925, oil and varnished water colour on panel,*
30¼" x 38⅝")
Arnesberg Collection, The Philadelphia Museum of
Fine Art. American Library Colour Slide Company.

French or Flemish Tapestry
The Hunt of the Unicorn VII
The Unicorn in Captivity
(*late 15th or early 16th century, silk and wool tapes-*
try, with silver threads).
from the Château of Verteuil.
The Metropolitan Museum of Art, New York, The
Cloisters Collection, Gift of John D. Rockefeller, 1937.

Giuseppe Arcimboldo (1527-1595, Italian)
Allegory of Water
(*oil colour on panel, 26⅜″ x 20″*)
Kunsthistorisches Museum, Wien (Vienna).

Edward Lear (1812-1888, English)
The Bird in the Bush
(*1846 edition of "A Book of Nonsense", pen
drawing*)
*illustration to Edward Lear's "A Book of Nonsense"
ed. by R. L. Megroz, Penguin Books, p. 89.*

There was an Old Man who said, 'Hush!
I perceive a young bird in this bush!'
When they said—'Is it small?' He replied—'Not at all!
It is four times as big as the bush!'